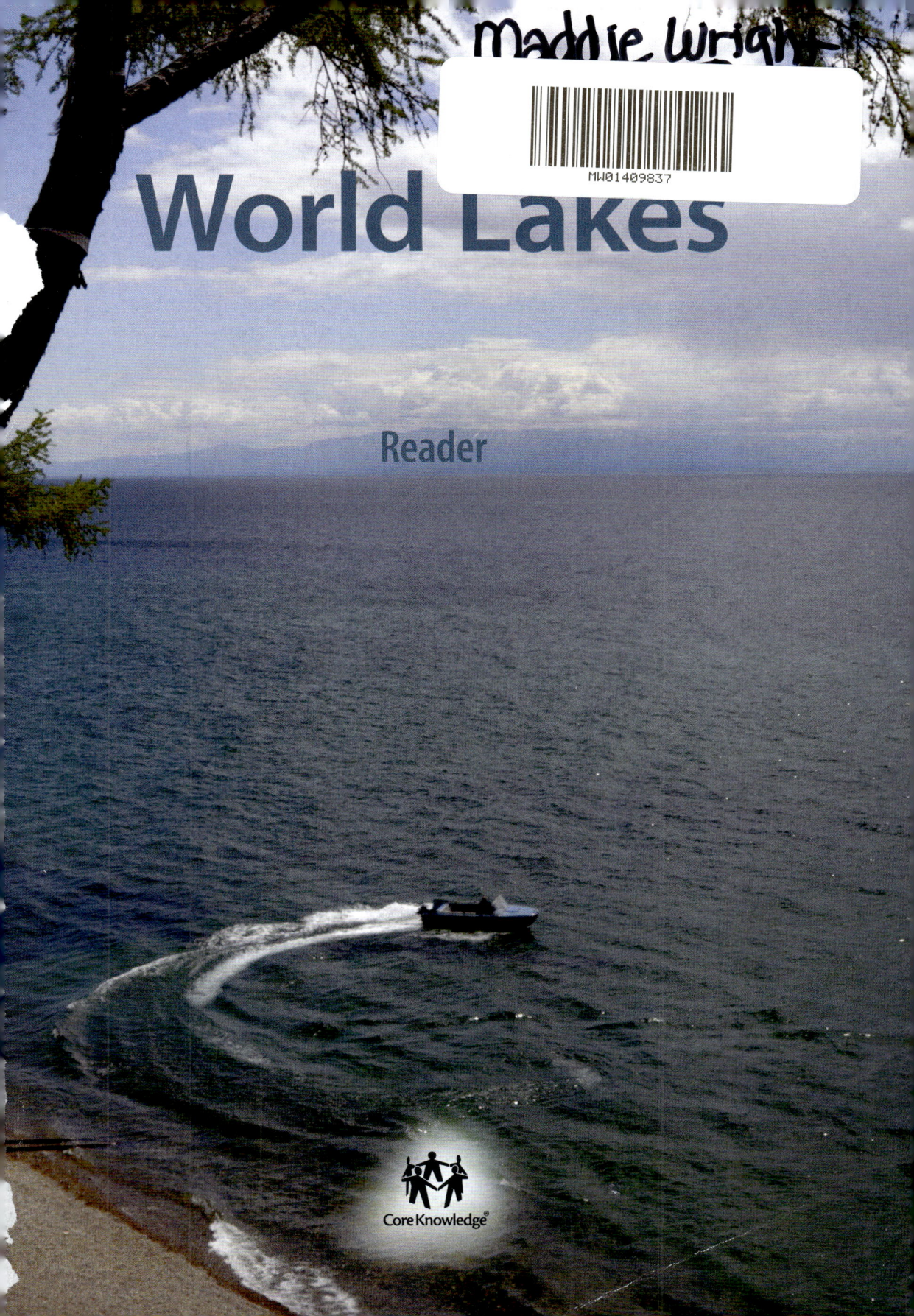
World Lakes

Reader

Copyright © 2017 Core Knowledge Foundation
www.coreknowledge.org

All Rights Reserved.

Core Knowledge®, Core Knowledge Curriculum Series™, Core Knowledge History and Geography™ and CKHG™ are trademarks of the Core Knowledge Foundation.

Trademarks and trade names are shown in this book strictly for illustrative and educational purposes and are the property of their respective owners. References herein should not be regarded as affecting the validity of said trademarks and trade names.

Printed in Canada

ISBN: 978-1-68380-058-3

World Lakes

Table of Contents

Chapter 1	**Lakes of Africa**	2
Chapter 2	**Lakes of South America**	12
Chapter 3	**The Great Lakes of North America**	18
Chapter 4	**Lakes of Eurasia**	28
Atlas		36
Glossary		40

World Lakes
Reader
Core Knowledge History and Geography™

Chapter 1
Lakes of Africa

Lake Tanganyika Ready? Your air tank is strapped on your back and ready to go. Set? You make sure your scuba mask is tight on your face, covering your eyes and nose. Your friend Stephanie gives you a smile. Go! Together you jump off the boat into the **lake**.

> **The Big Question**
>
> What resources and benefits does each of the three African lakes provide to people?

> **Vocabulary**
>
> **lake,** n. a body of water surrounded by land

You're scuba diving in Lake Tanganyika (/tan*guh*nee*kuh/), Africa's deepest and longest lake. You've come to the home of many of the tropical fish you've seen in the aquarium in your school.

The frontosa is a species of fish commonly found in Lake Tanganyika.

Lake Tanganyika is the longest freshwater lake in the world.

A cloud of shimmering colors swirls past Stephanie and moves slowly toward you. Suddenly shiny blues, bright golds, and neon greens sparkle all around you. You can practically hear Stephanie thinking, "Unbelievable!"

You stop and watch a thousand tiny fish darting around. Most of them are only as long as your finger, about two or three inches. Some fish are covered with bold black stripes. Others have polka dots on their backs and fins. These fish have strange names. Some are called *giraffes*. Others are called *zebras*, *daffodils*, *gold faces*, and *six-stripes*. Because of the unusual beauty of these fish, people all over the world pay hundreds of dollars to buy only one or two of them.

You could watch the fish for hours. You glance over at Stephanie. She motions upward, as if to say, "Let's go back up to the boat and get on with our trip!" You swim to the surface.

Back on the boat, you try to remember what else is unusual about Lake Tanganyika. You look at your map. Lake Tanganyika is one of a group of lakes that point like long fingers down the side of the map.

"Why are these lakes so long, deep, and narrow?" you ask Stephanie.

"They're in the **rift valley**," she answers. You both look across Lake Tanganyika toward the shore, where mountains rise up from the water's edge.

> **Vocabulary**
>
> **rift valley,** n. a long, deep, narrow valley in East Africa

"I read that many centuries ago," continued Stephanie, "Earth's surface cracked and began separating between those mountain ranges. Gradually the edges of the cracks pulled farther and farther away from each other. The ground between the edges dropped down many hundreds of feet, forming deep valleys that filled up with water to form the lakes."

Cool Facts About Lake Tanganyika
- Lake Tanganyika is Africa's second largest lake.
- Lake Tanganyika is the second deepest freshwater lake in the world.
- Lake Tanganyika is part of the border between eastern and central Africa.

"That's very interesting! Hey! I have an idea. Why don't we eat fish for dinner tonight?" you suggest to Stephanie. You don't mean the sparkling green and blue fish; you mean the bigger fish that people catch from this lake to eat. Fish are a valuable **resource** from Lake Tanganyika.

Lake Tanganyika is a long lake. It touches the boundaries of four different countries—Democratic Republic of the Congo, Tanzania, Burundi, and Zambia. This makes Lake Tanganyika a good **transportation route**. Along the lake's shores are several towns and small cities, with **docks** for ferryboats and fishing boats.

Vocabulary

resource, n. something that people can use

"transportation route," (phrase), a path for traveling from one place to another

dock, n. a platform where boats can load and unload people and goods

Major African Lakes

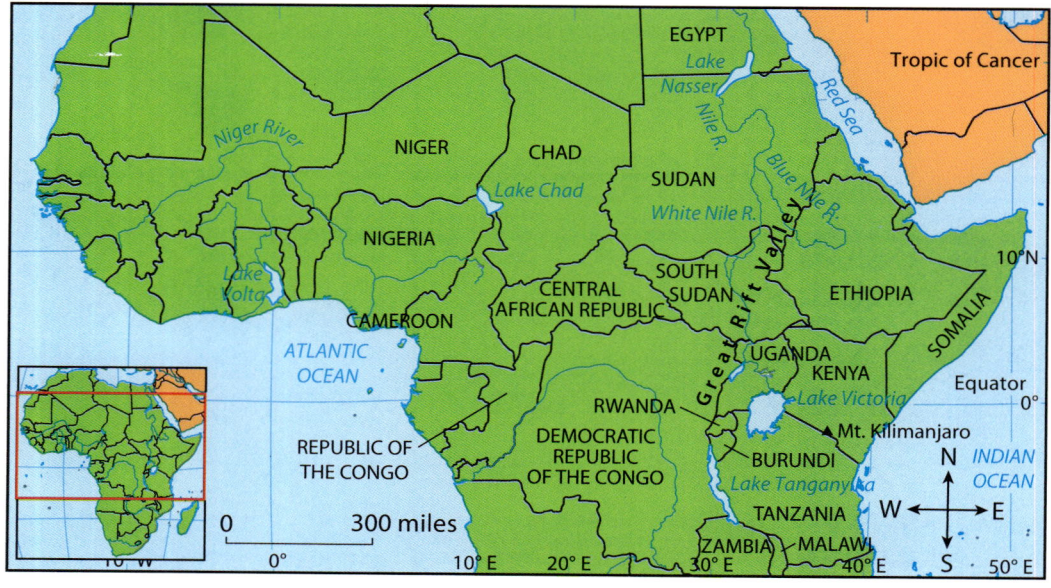

The map shows the three African lakes featured in this chapter.

"Fish for dinner, and then tomorrow we leave for Lake Victoria," Stephanie says.

Lake Victoria

Africa has many other large lakes. These lakes include Lake Nasser, Lake Volta, Lake Chad, and Lake Victoria. Lake Victoria is northeast of Lake Tanganyika. It's the largest lake in Africa. You and Stephanie have decided to visit Lake Victoria because it is the **source** of the famous Nile River. To get from Lake Tanganyika to Lake Victoria, you cross through the country of Tanzania (/tan*zuh*nee*uh/). First your jeep climbs up over the mountains along the edge of Lake Tanganyika. Then you cross the flat, grassy lands of Tanzania.

> **Vocabulary**
>
> **source,** n. a starting point or beginning of a river's water

You pass through many villages and towns. The road is often quite crowded with people, bicycles, and motor vehicles. People carry bundles or babies, talk with each other, and busily do errands.

Tanzania and its neighbor, Kenya, are famous for their **game reserves** and national parks. Tourists visit these parks to see elephants, giraffes, and other wildlife. Other tourists climb Mount Kilimanjaro (/kil*uh*man*jar*oe/), Africa's highest peak. Even though Lake Victoria is near these interesting places, probably few tourists see what you are about to see.

> **Vocabulary**
>
> **game reserve,** n. an area set aside by the government where animals are protected from hunters

"We really want to see where the Nile begins," you tell Paul, your guide. "In school we learned about the Nile River and how the ancient Egyptians built the pyramids near it."

"No problem!" Paul says. "Did you know that Lake Victoria is named for Queen Victoria of Great Britain? She was queen in the 1800s. That's when the first Europeans came to this lake," Paul continues.

Many beautiful islands dot this lake. Some of them are quite large. In one area steep cliffs rise from the shore. In another area the shore is more like a marsh or swamp. It takes you several days as you travel from the southern part of the lake in Tanzania to the northern part of the lake in Uganda. Finally, you reach the place where water drains out of Lake Victoria.

"Is this the beginning of the Nile River?" you ask.

"Actually, one of the small rivers that flows into Lake Victoria is the very beginning of the Nile River," Paul explains. "But the water flowing out of the lake is called the Victoria Nile River."

"The river is still quite small here," Paul says. "But by the time it gets to the country of South Sudan, it's much bigger. It's called the White Nile there."

"Yes," Stephanie nods, "I remember learning about the White Nile. In Sudan, it joins with the Blue Nile. The Blue Nile flows from Ethiopia (/ee*thee*oe*pee*uh/). Together they form the river called the Nile, the one that flows northward through Egypt."

"Right," Paul says. "The Nile is the longest river in the world. Here you are only at the beginning of it!"

Cool Facts About Lake Victoria

- Lake Victoria is Africa's largest lake.
- Lake Victoria is the largest tropical lake in the world.
- Lake Victoria is home to more than two hundred different kinds of fish, including the Nile perch, which can grow up to six feet in length, and weigh more than four hundred pounds.

Lake Chad

The last African lake on your tour, Lake Chad, is in western Africa. To get there, you have to fly from Uganda to Nigeria and then take a jeep to the lake. Like Lake Victoria and Lake Tanganyika,

Lake Chad is shared by several countries. Chad, Niger, Nigeria, and Cameroon each touch the shores of Lake Chad.

"This is really different from the other lakes we saw," Stephanie says. "It's not mountainous here, and the weather is pretty dry." You look at the land around the lake. It's mostly flat. The bright sun overhead makes the air very hot, about 100°F.

"But," you remind her, "people have lived around this lake for thousands of years."

Two men in a fishing boat stop and ask if you need directions. They're brothers who make their living from catching and selling fish. The brothers, Abdul and Moussa, know the lake well.

"Lake Chad is very shallow," Abdul says.

Fishing in Lake Chad provides a living for many people in the area.

"It is deeper from June to September," says Moussa. "That's our rainy season."

"Look over there," Abdul says. He points to the edge of the lake near where you are standing. "It looks like solid ground, doesn't it?"

> **Vocabulary**
>
> **papyrus,** n. a tall grasslike plant that grows in swamps or wetland areas

You nod in agreement. The area is completely covered with reeds and other plants.

"It's not solid ground," Moussa says. "Those are **papyrus** and cattails. They're actually growing in shallow water, right in the lake."

"Now look out there toward the middle of the lake," Abdul says. You see some places where the water's surface looks rough and lumpy with spots of color.

"What is that?" Stephanie asks.

"Waterlilies," says Moussa. "Hundreds of them. They're so crowded together that they form a mat that is almost solid."

Like Abdul and Moussa, many people make their living by fishing in the lake. Others have farms or graze livestock nearby. But it's fish that you see for sale everywhere. In fish markets, on the docks, and along the streets, people sell dried fish, fresh fish, salted fish, and smoked fish.

Cool Facts About Lake Chad

- Lake Chad is getting smaller. Six thousand years ago, Lake Chad was twenty times bigger!

- Farming is becoming more difficult around Lake Chad. The lake's water used to support neighboring farmland. As the lake has shrunk, the water available for farming has become scarce. This water shortage affects thousands of people.

Chapter 2
Lakes of South America

Lake Titicaca Our train chugged across the flat plateau of southern Peru. In the distance, I could see the snow-covered peaks of the Andes in Peru and Bolivia.

> **The Big Question**
>
> In what ways are these South American lakes important natural resources?

> **Vocabulary**
>
> **natural resource,** n. something from nature that is useful to humans
>
> **plateau,** n. a large area of high, flat ground

I was writing postcards after visiting Lake Titicaca (/tit*ih*kah*kuh/), one of the world's highest lakes. Lake Titicaca is located high in the Andes. It is bordered by the countries of Peru and Bolivia.

I asked my Peruvian friend, Ricardo, what I should write. I was visiting Ricardo for several weeks. He used to go to my school when he lived in the United States. I was happy that I could visit with him and that we could explore some of the lakes of South America together.

"You should tell your friends at home about the ruins we saw," Ricardo suggested.

Now that was interesting! Huge stone ruins stand on the shores of Lake Titicaca. They were left by a civilization that lived in the area

People living near Lake Titicaca use boats made of reeds to travel on the lake.

hundreds of years before the Inca. Standing among the ancient stones, I had imagined what it looked like thousands of years ago.

"What about those llamas (/lah*muz/) we ran into?" Ricardo asked.

Llamas are animals that are like camels but smaller. One had looked me straight in the eye. They have really long necks, sort of like short giraffes. Farmers near Lake Titicaca raise llamas for the animals' wool. The farmers fasten ribbons or tiny bells onto the llamas' ears to show who owns them. Everywhere I went, I saw people selling colorful goods made from llama wool. I saw llama-wool sweaters, scarves, hats, gloves, and blankets. They come in handy at night when it gets very cold.

"Tell them you ate a lot of *papas*," Ricardo continued.

In South America, people use llamas for carrying goods, and they use their wool, too!

That's what they call potatoes in Peru and Bolivia. The cool climate near Lake Titicaca is great for growing potatoes. People who live around the lake grow many different kinds. In fact, the first potatoes in the world were grown in this part of South America. We wouldn't have the french fries all of us enjoy today if it weren't for those first *papas*.

"And don't forget the lake!" Ricardo said.

That's right! We took a short cruise on Lake Titicaca. We saw that people get practically everything they need from the lake. They get fish to eat, water for their crops, and of course water to drink. The reeds that grow in the lake are incredibly strong. People make furniture, roofs, and even boats with them.

Find Lakes Titicaca and Maracaibo on this map. Notice that Lake Titicaca is completely surrounded by land, but Lake Maracaibo has an outlet to the Caribbean Sea.

Cool Facts About Lake Titicaca

- More than twenty-five rivers feed into Lake Titicaca.
- Lake Titicaca's water comes from melting glaciers and rainwater.
- No one knows for certain what Lake Titicaca's name means.

Lake Maracaibo

A few days later, Ricardo and I traveled to Venezuela. There we visited Lake Maracaibo (/mar*uh*kie*boe/), one of the most important lakes in South America. We discovered that Lake Maracaibo is not really a lake. It is not completely surrounded by land. Instead it is a **gulf**.

The area is rich with **petroleum** deposits under Lake Maracaibo's waters, along its shores, and out along the Atlantic Coast. We saw oil **derricks** in the water and oil tankers on the water. There were oil storage tanks on the land and oil company offices in many places.

"You should tell your friends about how important petroleum, or oil, is in Venezuela," Ricardo suggested.

"Yes, I could tell them that," I say.

"Remember what products are made with petroleum?" Ricardo asks.

> **Vocabulary**
>
> **gulf,** n. a part of an ocean extending into land
>
> **petroleum,** n. a naturally occurring oil found in certain rock layers under Earth's surface used to make plastics and fuels, such as gasoline
>
> **derrick,** n. a framework tower that supports a drill over an oil well

"Sure! Petroleum is used in all kinds of everyday goods: plastic, paint, gasoline, cosmetics, and fabrics," I answer. "I could also explain how the city of Maracaibo has grown. It now has many different **industries**."

"That's right," Ricardo agreed. "The growth of the city is largely due to petroleum."

Lake Maracaibo is different from Lake Titicaca. Lake Titicaca is a quiet lake where people make their living farming and fishing. Lake Maracaibo is a bustling **trading hub** and center of industry.

> **Vocabulary**
>
> **industry,** n. a business that manufactures a product or provides a service
>
> **"trading hub,"** (phrase), a place that is a center for the buying and selling of goods and services

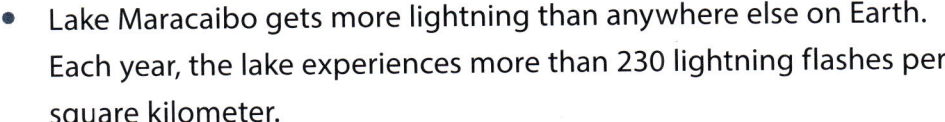

Cool Facts About Lake Maracaibo
- Lake Maracaibo gets more lightning than anywhere else on Earth. Each year, the lake experiences more than 230 lightning flashes per square kilometer.

Chapter 3
The Great Lakes of North America

A Shipwreck Icy winds roared across the lake. A ship as long as two football fields struggled. Enormous waves washed over the ship's deck. Late in the afternoon the ship's captain radioed to say that the ship was taking on heavy waters.

> **The Big Question**
>
> Why are the Great Lakes of North America such important transportation routes?

The crew of a nearby ship was watching this ship, which was carrying thousands of tons of **minerals**. At 7:10 p.m. the captain radioed to say that the ship was holding its own.

But five minutes later, the ship had simply vanished. Afterward, a rescue team found it on the floor of the lake, broken in half. The captain and all the crew members died.

> **Vocabulary**
>
> **mineral,** n. a naturally-occurring substance found in Earth's crust.

This shipwreck occurred in 1975. People were shocked. How could such a disaster happen?

For one thing, the SS *Edmund Fitzgerald* was sailing on Lake Superior, the largest lake in the United States. Lake Superior is a very pleasant

The SS *Edmund Fitzgerald* sank during a powerful storm on Lake Superior in 1975.

place to sail and fish in the summer. In the winter, though, this lake experiences wild storms and hurricane-force winds. Even the largest and heaviest ships can be tossed around. The area where the shipwreck occurred is sometimes called the Graveyard of Ships.

Investigators discovered that a cover door over the ship's cargo area had collapsed. Then water from the crashing waves flooded inside the ship.

Locks and Straits

What do crews on ships such as the SS *Edmund Fitzgerald* see as they cross the Great Lakes? To find out, my friend Tameeka and I asked the captain of a large sailboat to take us on a journey around Lake Superior, Lake Michigan, Lake Huron, Lake Erie, and Lake Ontario. These five lakes not only provide drinking water, they are also used for fishing, shipping, and for recreation. Our trip will take several weeks. We ask the captain to point out the most interesting places along the way.

Each lake is so large that when you stand along the shore and look across the water, you cannot see the other side of the lake. It's almost like looking out at the ocean. The captain points far out across the water. Tameeka and I squint and look hard. Finally we see a bump on the flat gray horizon. We might not have seen it if the captain hadn't pointed it out. The captain says, "That little bump out there is probably a very large ship. A lot of huge **cargo ships** travel on

> **Vocabulary**
>
> "cargo ship," n. a large boat used to carry goods

the Great Lakes. They carry grain, iron ore, steel, timber, and other products to and from port cities along the lakes."

Sooner or later nearly all the big ships on Lake Superior have to go through Sault Ste Marie (/soo/saint/muh*ree/), Michigan. That's where the ships use a canal to get from Lake Superior to Lake Huron. On this windy day, our sailboat arrives at Sault Ste Marie quickly. The canal has a series of **locks**, sections of the canal that are closed off with gates. The captain explains how they work.

> **Vocabulary**
>
> **canal,** n. a channel dug by people, used by boats or for irrigation
>
> **lock,** n. a part of a canal that has gates for lowering and raising the water level

"Locks help a ship move from a lake where the surface of the water is high, such as Lake Superior, to a lower lake, such as Lake Huron,"

Cargo ships use the locks at Sault Ste Marie to travel from Lake Superior to Lake Huron.

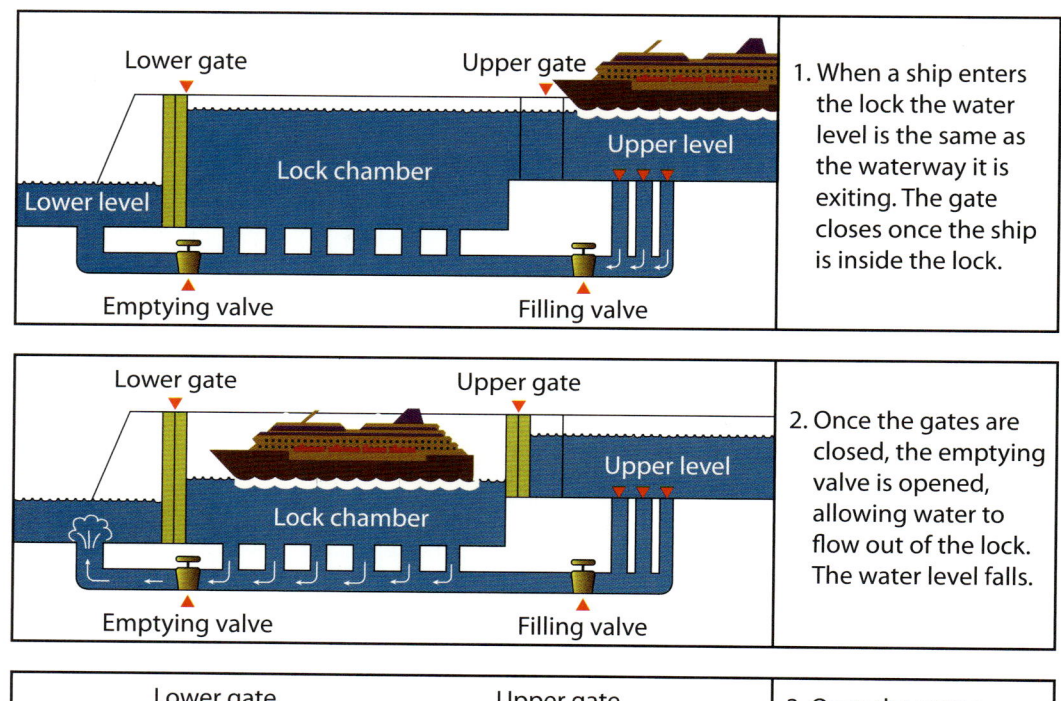

1. When a ship enters the lock the water level is the same as the waterway it is exiting. The gate closes once the ship is inside the lock.

2. Once the gates are closed, the emptying valve is opened, allowing water to flow out of the lock. The water level falls.

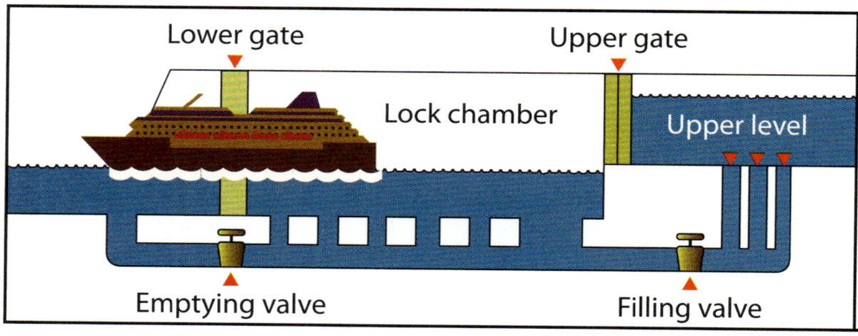

3. Once the water reaches the level of the lower water level, the valve is closed. The gate is opened and the ship moves out into the waterway.

Locks help ships move between two bodies of water at different heights.

he says. Our sailboat leaves Lake Superior, and we enter the first lock. The gates shut behind us. We feel a little nudge as our sailboat stops. We hear a lot of rushing water. Then the sailboat begins moving downward very, very slowly.

"Don't worry!" the captain says. "We're not sinking! Some of the water in the lock is being removed. This lowers the water level so that it matches the water level in the next lock."

Then the gates in front of us open. Our boat moves into the next lock. After going through a number of locks, our sailboat is in lower water. We enter Lake Huron. The whole process took less than an hour.

Next, the captain takes us to another interesting part of the Great Lakes, the Straits of Mackinac (/mack*in*awe/).

> **Vocabulary**
> **strait,** n. a narrow body of water that connects two larger bodies of water

(A **strait** is a narrow body of water that connects two larger bodies of water.) Ships and boats pass through this waterway to get from Lake Huron to Lake Michigan.

Tameeka and I want to see the Straits of Mackinac from one of the most famous bridges in America, the Mackinac Bridge. This is among the longest bridges ever built. It is one of the strongest, too. It has to survive the ice and winter winds of the Great Lakes. The captain docks the sailboat, and we drive the five miles across the bridge. Through the window we see water everywhere. We also see islands, a ferryboat, and some sailboats. The body of

The Mackinac Bridge, one of the longest bridges ever built, crosses the Straits of Mackinac.

water is not nearly as wide as one of the Great Lakes; therefore ships have to move more carefully.

Sailing on Lake Michigan and Lake Huron

Back on the sailboat, the captain has brought us to Lake Michigan, the only Great Lake entirely inside the United States. We head toward the other end of the lake, to Chicago, Illinois.

There, products are loaded onto ships and carried to other cities on the Great Lakes or through the Great Lakes to the ocean. Chicago is an important inland port in America.

After admiring the Chicago skyline, we head north. We pass under the Mackinac Bridge again and enter Lake Huron. The captain asks us a question.

"Did you ever notice that the southern part of Michigan is shaped like a mitten?"

Tameeka and I look at a map. Michigan *does* look like a mitten! Lake Huron makes that possible. Michigan's "thumb" and "index finger" are separated by Saginaw Bay, a large bay of Lake Huron. The main part of the lake continues south toward the next of the Great Lakes, Lake Erie.

The captain gives us a riddle. "Name a large U.S. city on the Great Lakes from which you can travel south to get to Canada."

We're puzzled. Tameeka checks the map again.

"Detroit, Michigan!" Tameeka shouts. Detroit is a large industrial city built on the Detroit River, between Lake Huron and Lake Erie.

Map of the Great Lakes

The Great Lakes border eight U.S. states, as well as a number of Canadian provinces, and provide a way for these states and provinces to ship their products by water.

"And what is Detroit's nickname?" the captain asks. I remember that ships carry iron ore and steel across the Great Lakes. Many of these materials are shipped to cities, such as Gary, Indiana. The automobile industry began near Detroit. That's how the city got its nickname. "Motor City!" I shout. The captain gives up trying to stump us, at least for a while.

Two Lakes and a Waterfall

We've sailed past Detroit, and now we're in Lake Erie, the shallowest of the Great Lakes. Along the shore are **smokestacks**, lighthouses, office towers, and loading

> **Vocabulary**
>
> **smokestack**, n. a tall chimney on a factory or ship

docks. These are in some of the important industrial cities, such as Cleveland, Ohio. Finally we reach Buffalo, New York. Here we leave our sailboat for a day to visit the great Niagara Falls, one of the world's largest waterfalls. The falls are created by the Niagara River, which flows from Lake Erie into Lake Ontario.

"How will you get the sailboat over Niagara Falls?" Tameeka asks the captain. He laughs and gets out the map again.

"I'm going to take this boat around the falls, down the Welland Canal," he says. "If I took the boat over Niagara Falls, you might never see me or the boat again! Luckily the canal allows ships to travel between Lake Erie and Lake Ontario."

When we get to Niagara Falls, we see what he means. A giant wall of water crashes over a huge cliff. The roar of the falls is so loud we can

Niagara Falls has two parts: American Falls and Horseshoe Falls. This photo shows a tour boat approaching Horseshoe Falls.

hardly hear each other. On our tour-boat ride along the bottom of the falls, everyone wears raincoats. The spray gets us wet anyway!

On Lake Ontario we again meet the captain and board the sailboat. The day is sunny, and the wind is brisk. We almost fly along the water, feeling the wind tugging at the sails. The captain points out rows of trees along the shore. They are apple, peach, and cherry trees.

Finally our journey is over. The captain says that up ahead is the St. Lawrence Seaway, which connects Lake Ontario to the St. Lawrence River. The river flows into the Atlantic Ocean. Cargo ships are able to use the lakes, locks, canals, the seaway, and the river to travel from Lake Superior all the way to the Atlantic Ocean.

Tameeka and I say goodbye to the captain. He's become our friend.

"The Great Lakes really are pretty great," he says. And we agree.

Cool Facts About the Great Lakes

- Lake Superior is so deep, the water of the other four great lakes would fit inside!
- Ten percent of Earth's unfrozen fresh water is in Lake Superior.
- Beneath Lake Huron there are ancient structures believed to be nine thousand years old.
- In the 1800s, pirates were a regular threat on Lake Michigan.
- The lake on Saturn's moon Titan is named after Lake Ontario.

Chapter 4
Lakes of Eurasia

Lake Baikal "Be careful! Don't lean over so far!" Valentin shouts. He is my guide on Russia's Lake Baikal (/bie*kahl/). "You'll fall out of the boat!"

> **The Big Question**
>
> Why do some lakes contain fresh water and some salt water?

"I just want some of those pebbles on the bottom of the lake," I explain.

Valentin laughs. "You'll never reach them. Those pebbles may look like they're just below the surface, but really they are many feet away. And they're probably not pebbles."

> **Vocabulary**
>
> **optical illusion,** n. something that appears to be different from what it really is

Valentin sees my expression of disbelief. He explains. He tells me that Lake Baikal is a very deep lake—the deepest in the world. It's also a very clear lake. Because it is so clear, things seem closer to the surface than they really are. It's an **optical illusion** (/op*tik*uhl/ il*oo*zhun/).

"Those 'little pebbles' you saw are probably huge rocks," Valentin laughs. "But don't feel bad. Everybody makes this mistake when they first visit here."

Lake Baikal in Siberia, Russia, is the deepest lake in the world.

Valentin tells our tour group many interesting facts about Lake Baikal. For instance, this one lake contains enough water to fill all five of the Great Lakes until they overflow.

Lake Baikal is sometimes called the Pearl of Siberia. That's because it's located in a region of Russia called Siberia. And, like a pearl, the lake is a great treasure to Russians. People also call this lake "the sacred lake" or "the sacred water." They believe it is mysterious, magical, and majestic. Lake Baikal is so deep that people imagine it has great mysteries down below.

Cool Facts About Lake Baikal
- Lake Baikal contains twenty percent of the world's unfrozen fresh water.
- The water in Lake Baikal is the most transparent of all the freshwater lakes in the world.

The land surrounding Lake Baikal is also a great natural treasure. Many Russians feel that the natural beauty around Lake Baikal is magical. High cliffs and forest-covered mountains rise above the lake. Reindeer, elk, deer, and bears live in the dense woods. Wild rivers empty their waters into the lake. Parks and game reserves around Lake Baikal protect the rivers and animals.

Things may not stay this wild and natural forever. Timber companies are cutting down some of the forest to make lumber and paper. Ships are built on the lake's shore, and fishing boats come and go. A railroad connects mines and industries to towns along the shore.

For now, I am happy to breathe the fresh air and imagine the mysteries at the bottom of the world's deepest lake.

Major Lakes of Eurasia

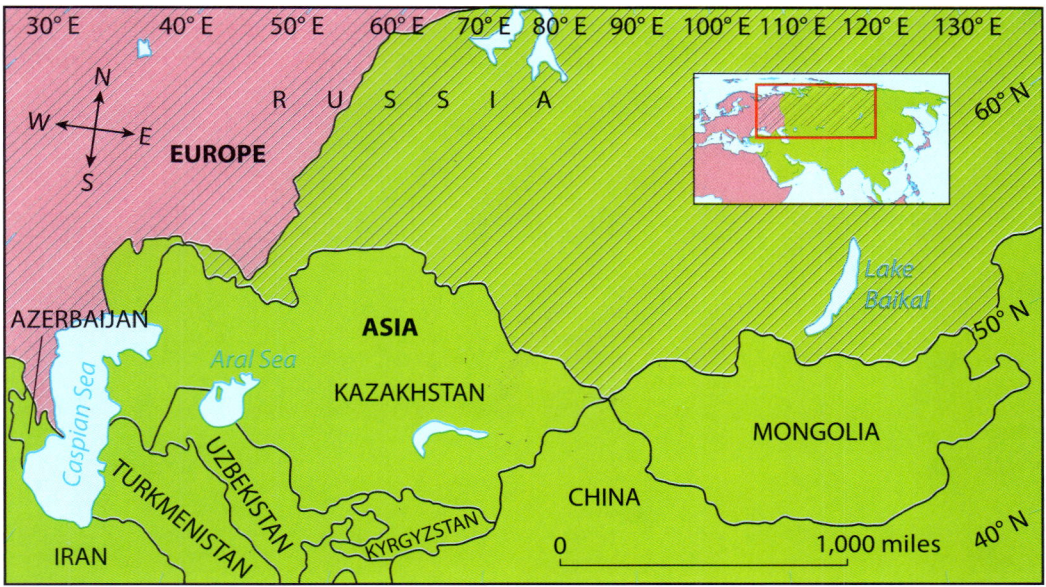

Use the scale of miles on this map to measure the distances between the Caspian Sea, the Aral Sea, and Lake Baikal.

The Caspian Sea

Most of the world's lakes are freshwater lakes, but a few contain salt water. A lake has salt water if its water **evaporates** more quickly than rivers or rain can bring in new water. When water evaporates, it leaves behind salts and other minerals.

> **Vocabulary**
>
> **evaporate,** v. to change a liquid to a vapor or gas
>
> **outlet,** n. a stream that flows out of a larger body of water

You can see how this works on a hot summer day. If you let the sweat on your arm evaporate and then lick your arm, your skin will taste a little salty.

Fresh water comes into the Caspian Sea from a number of streams and lakes. The sea has salt water because it has no **outlet**. The Caspian Sea (which is really a lake) is located in a very dry climate.

31

Oil derricks are a common sight on the Caspian Sea.

Its water evaporates, leaving behind salt and other minerals. After thousands of years, a lot of salt has built up in the Caspian Sea.

The Caspian Sea is a very large body of water. It has long been a good trade route. In the past, traders traveled between lands far to the east in Asia and lands far to the west in Europe. Many traders carried their goods by boat or ship across this lake during their travels.

Then people discovered how valuable oil is. Some of the world's largest oil deposits are located around and under the Caspian Sea. The Caspian Sea became more than just a trade route.

Cool Facts About the Caspian Sea
- The Caspian Sea is the world's largest inland body of water.
- The Caspian Sea is the largest saltwater lake in the world.

The Aral Sea

From the Caspian Sea, our group travels to the next stop on our trip, the Aral Sea. Sadly, the Aral Sea is shrinking. The **volume** of the lake has decreased by ninety percent in the past few decades. The Aral Sea is a saltwater lake in the Central Asian nations of Uzbekistan and Kazakhstan.

> **Vocabulary**
>
> **volume,** n. the amount of space that something fills
>
> **divert,** v. to change the path of a river

The Aral Sea was once the fourth largest lake in the world. Now its shoreline has receded up to seventy-five miles in places; the sea level has dropped more than fifty feet. The southeastern part of the lake has dried up completely.

I ask our new guide, Kodir, what caused this.

"Unfortunately this was not a natural change," he answers. "People **diverted** rivers that flowed into the Aral Sea. They needed the water to grow cotton crops for export. A canal was planned to guide water from other rivers into the sea, but the canal was never built."

The Shrinking of the Aral Sea

This map shows how the Aral Sea has shrunk from the world's fourth largest lake to almost nothing.

This boat was left high and dry on the Aral Sea as the waters in the lake receded.

"How does the shrinking of the lake affect the people who live nearby?" we ask.

Kodir explains that the shrinking of this lake has affected the climate. Snow comes earlier each year. Spring comes later. The growing season is shorter. Also, people who used to live on the shore now live miles and miles away from the water. Many people who relied on fishing can no longer do so.

"What will happen to the Aral Sea and the region around it?" we ask.

"No one knows for sure," Kodir replies. "Five Central Asian nations are affected by the changes in the sea. But the problem may be too big to solve."

Cool Facts About the Aral Sea
- The Aral Sea was once the same size as West Virginia.
- The two rivers that fed into the Aral Sea also supported towns along the Silk Road, a trade route between Europe and China.

What Is a Lake?

We have visited many large bodies of water. Some are called lakes. Some are called seas. Now we ask Kodir a question that has been on our minds for a while: "If a lake can be salty or called a sea, like the Aral Sea and the Caspian Sea, and a gulf can be called a lake like Lake Maracaibo in South America, then how can we recognize a real lake?"

Kodir laughs. "That is a really good question. Even experts have some difficulty telling lakes from seas. One definition of a lake is a body of water surrounded by land. But the Great Lakes of North America are not completely surrounded by land. The St. Lawrence River connects them to the Atlantic Ocean. Both the Black Sea and the Mediterranean Sea are almost completely surrounded by land, but few experts would call them lakes. So it's tricky to distinguish between lakes and seas. If you want to find out if a body of water is considered a lake by experts, an almanac or encyclopedia can help you. Don't be surprised to find differences of opinion, though."

We think about what Kodir and Valentin have shown us and told us. We realize that no matter what they are called, these bodies of water are very important. They are sources of fish and other foods. They provide water for crops. They are used as transportation routes for people and goods. They provide opportunities for fun and relaxation. Whether they are freshwater or saltwater, large or small, lakes are very important geographic features of Earth.

Atlas

Major African Lakes

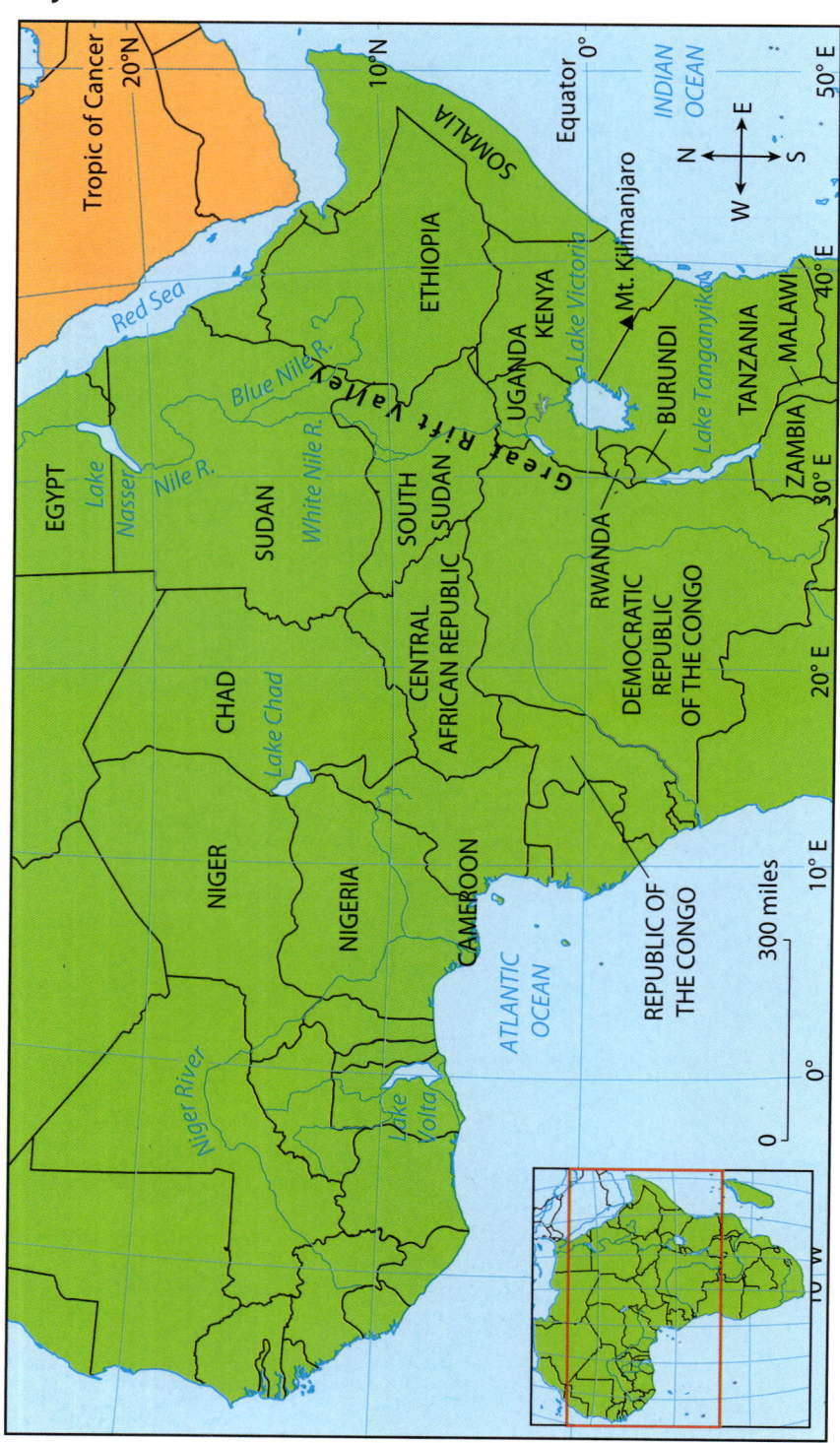

Atlas

Lakes and Rivers of South America

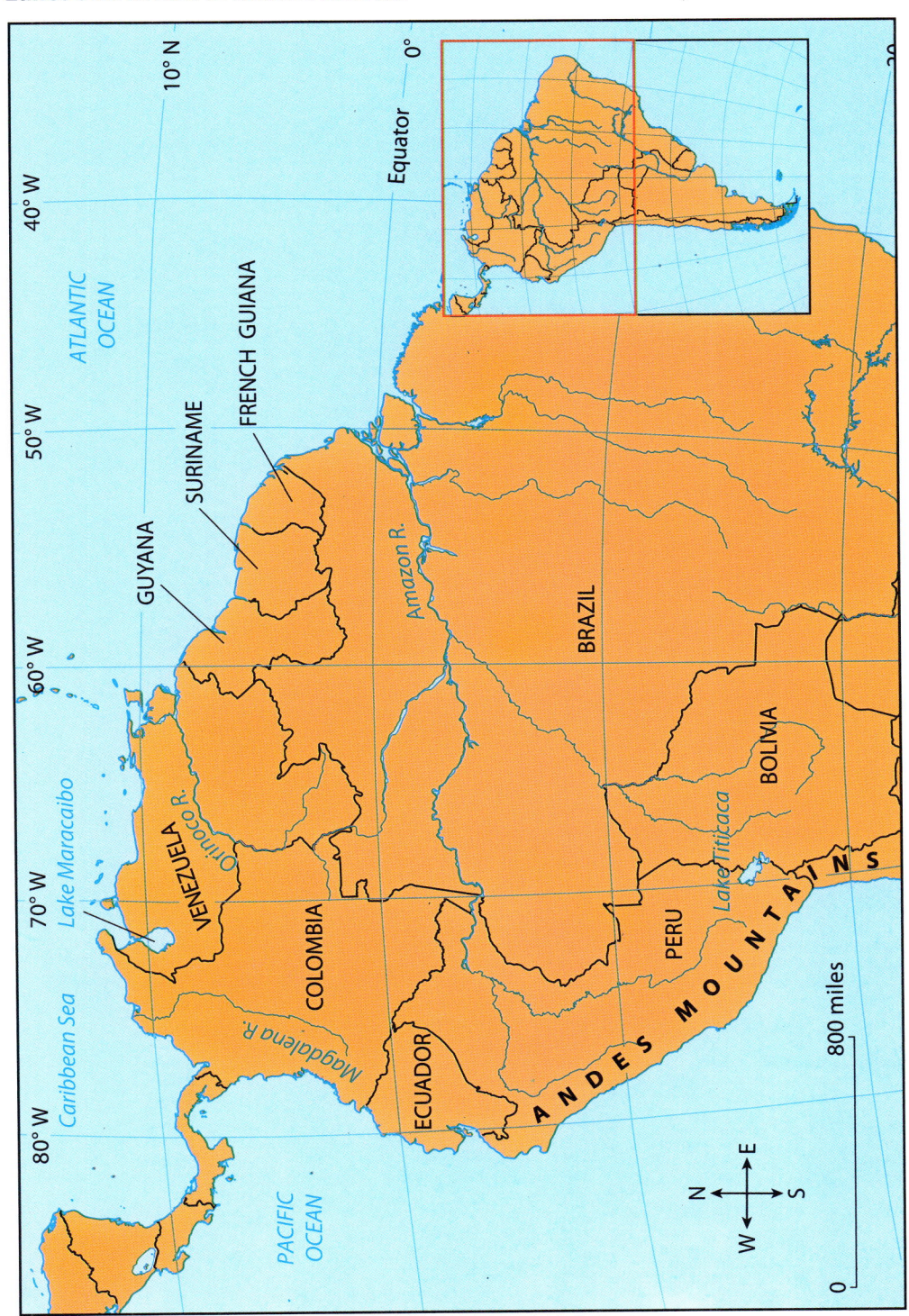

Atlas

Map of the Great Lakes

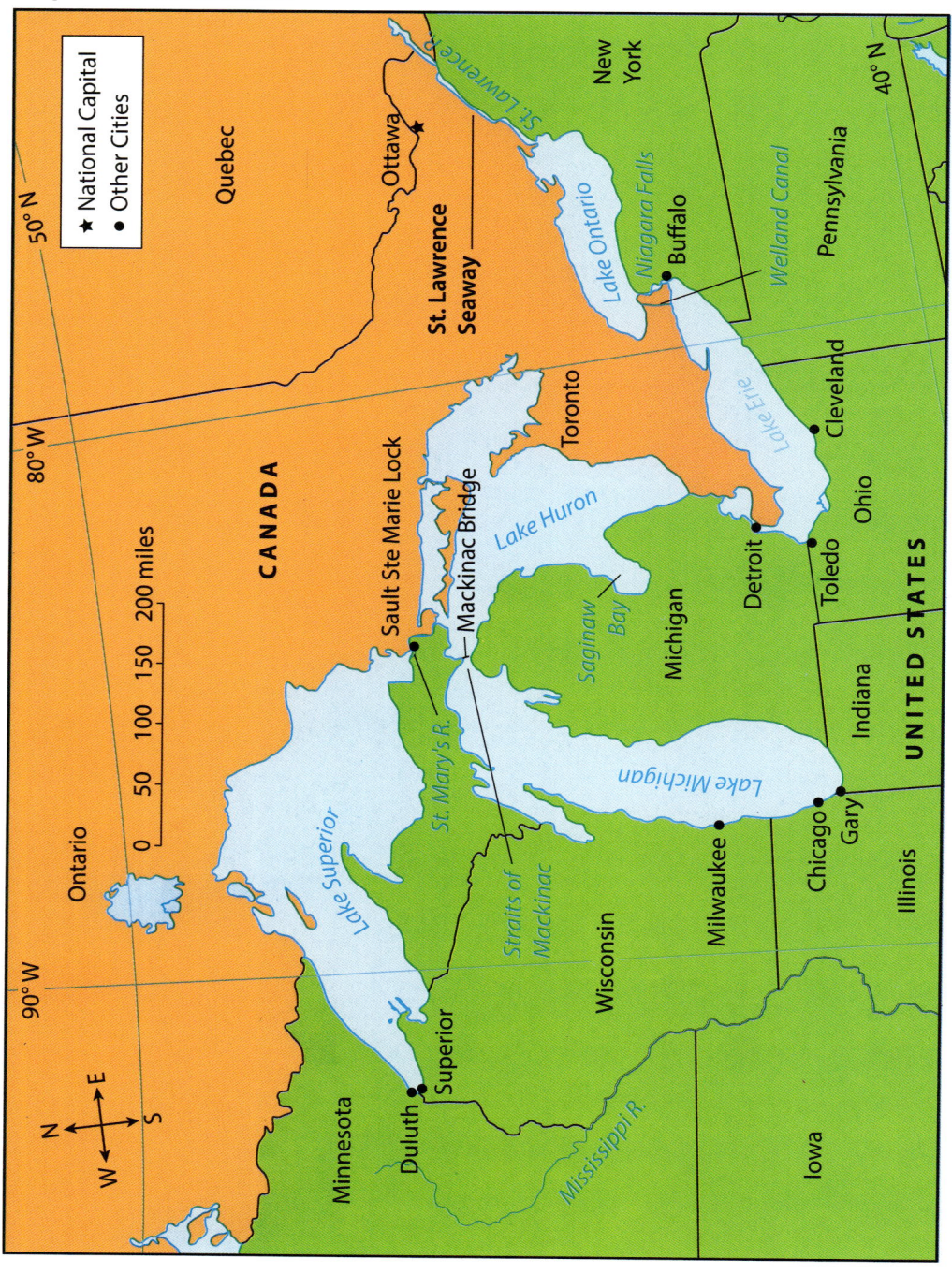

Atlas

Major Lakes of Eurasia

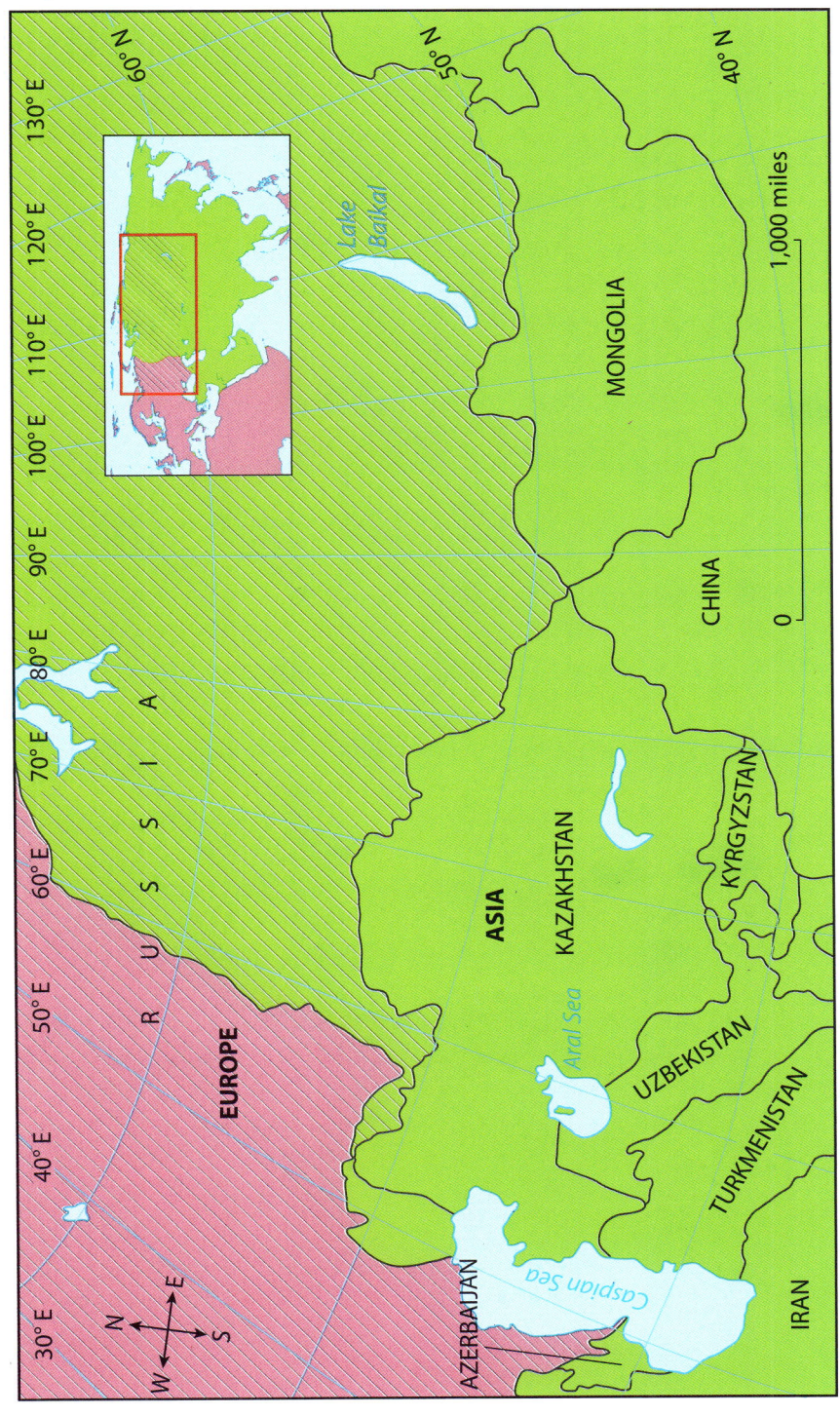

Glossary

C

canal, n. a channel dug by people, used by boats or for irrigation (21)

"cargo ship," (phrase), a large boat used to carry goods (20)

D

derrick, n. a framework tower that supports a drill over an oil well (16)

divert, v. to change the path of a river (33)

dock, n. a platform where boats can load and unload people and goods (5)

E

evaporate, v. to change a liquid to a vapor or gas (31)

G

game reserve, n. an area set aside by the government where animals are protected from hunters (7)

gulf, n. a part of an ocean extending into land (16)

I

industry, n. a business that manufactures a product or provides a service (17)

L

lake, n. a body of water surrounded by land (2)

lock, n. a part of a canal that has gates for lowering and raising the water level (21)

M

mineral, n. a naturally-occurring substance found in Earth's crust. (18)

N

natural resource, n. something from nature that is useful to humans (12)

O

optical illusion, n. something that appears to be different from what it really is (28)

outlet, n. a stream that flows out of a larger body of water (31)

P

papyrus, n. a tall grasslike plant that grows in swamps or wetland areas (10)

petroleum, n. a naturally occurring oil found in certain rock layers under Earth's surface used to make plastics and fuels, such as gasoline (16)

plateau, n. a large area of high, flat ground (12)

R

resource, n. something that people can use (5)

rift valley, n. a long, deep, narrow valley in East Africa (4)

S

smokestack, n. a tall chimney on a factory or ship (25)

source, n. starting point or beginning of a river's water (6)

strait, n. a narrow body of water that connects two larger bodies of water (23)

T

"trading hub," (phrase), a place that is a center for the buying and selling of goods and services (17)

"transportation route," (phrase), a path for traveling from one place to another (5)

V

volume, n. the amount of space that something fills (33)

CKHG™
Core Knowledge History and Geography™

Series Editor-In-Chief
E.D. Hirsch, Jr.

Subject Matter Expert
Charles F. Gritzner, PhD, Distinguished Professor Emeritus of Geography, South Dakota State University

Illustration and Photo Credits
age fotostock/age fotostock/SuperStock: Cover C, 21
Blend Images/Superstock: 3
Eye Ubiquitous/Eye Ubiquitous/SuperStock: 1, 9
imageBROKER/imageBROKER/SuperStock: 23
Jean Michel Labat/ardea.com/ Pantheon/Superstock: Cover A, 3
Radius/Radius/SuperStock: 26
robertharding/robertharding/SuperStock: i, iii, 29
Sandro Di Carlo Darsa/ès/Superstock: 34
Seth Resnick/Seth Resnick/SuperStock: 14
Steve Vidler/Steve Vidler/SuperStock: Cover B, 12–13
United States Army Corps of Engineers/Wikimedia Commons 18–19
Wolfgang Kaehler/Wolfgang/Superstcok: 32